★ CONTENTS ★

ENDORSEMENTS

Adam Hamilton
SENIOR PASTOR, UNITED
METHODIST CHURCH
OF THE RESURRECTION,
LEAWOOD, KANSAS

Matthew Hartsfield
LEAD PASTOR, VAN DYKE
UNITED METHODIST CHURCH,
LUTZ, FLORIDA

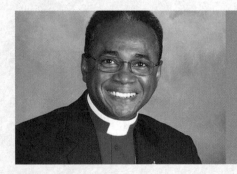

James King
RETIRED BISHOP OF THE SOUTH
GEORGIA CONFERENCE OF THE
UNITED METHODIST CHURCH

"Jim and Jennifer are remarkable people whose love for Christ is evident to all who know them. Their ministry has touched tens of thousands of people. Their new study, *Hand Me Downs,* is focused on helping Christians experience a deeper faith and pass it on to future generations. As a parent and now a grandparent, leaving my children and granddaughter a legacy of faith is the one goal that matters most to me. *Hand Me Downs* is an important resource in helping to fulfill this goal."

"Jim and Jennifer Cowart are warm and engaging communicators who bring the Bible to life. I'm so excited they and their team have produced *Hand Me Downs.* This is a positive and practical experience which helps people enter into thoughtful reflection, leading to a healthy atmosphere for action and life change. Jim and Jennifer are the real deal. Their powerful teaching and ministry leadership are a sincere expression of their authentic relationship with Jesus Christ. Throughout our years of friendship, I have personally benefited from their natural hand-me-downs of love, grace, and faithfulness."

"Want to get better? *Hand Me Downs* has been created by Jim and Jennifer Cowart to help you grow in your faith through a small group experience as you live into the fullness of God's plan for your life. This is a fresh new way to get small groups together to easily focus on the word of God and discuss with others how the teaching session connects with where you are and how you can continue to grow as you seek to grow closer to God through Jesus Christ."

Welcome to *Hand Me Downs!*

When you hear the term *hand-me-downs*, you may think of worn-out shoes passed down by your sister or your brother's old broken-down bike that you were given as a kid. That is one form of a hand-me-down, but in this study we're going to focus on a more far-reaching kind—the spiritual hand-me-downs that are passed down from generation to generation.

During the next six weeks you'll have the chance to reflect on the faith heritage you've received, whether strong or weak, and then determine the legacy you want to leave for others. You will also have opportunities to share your own ideas and experiences, watch a short video teaching on that week's theme, discuss scriptures, and determine how you will apply what God is teaching you. As a special bonus, we hope that you will be building friendships with those in your group.

At the end of each chapter, you will find Daily Devotions with space for you to create your own plan of action in how you will apply what you're learning. We hope that you will take the time to slow down over these six weeks and allow God to speak to you about the legacy you are creating. By participating in this study, you will be learning with a large group in church, a small group in a living room, and alone during your daily quiet time.

We're excited about what God has in store for you and your group over the next few weeks, and we're praying that you will experience God in a fresh new way as a result of this study.

Blessings,
Jim and Jen

USING THIS PARTICIPANT GUIDE

TOOLS TO HELP YOU HAVE A GREAT SMALL GROUP EXPERIENCE!

Pray before each session—for your group members, for your time together, and for wisdom and insights.

1. Notice in the contents there are three sections: (1) Sessions, (2) Appendices, and (3) Community Group Leaders. Familiarize yourself with the appendices. Some of them will be used in the sessions themselves.

2. If you are facilitating/leading or coleading a community group, the Community Group Leaders section will give you some hard-learned experiences of others that will encourage you and help you avoid many common obstacles to effective community group leadership.

3. Use this workbook as a guide, not a straightjacket. If the group responds to the session in an unexpected but honest way, go with that. If you think of a better question than the next one in the lesson, ask it. Take to heart the insights included in the Frequent Questions pages and the Community Group Leaders section.

4. Enjoy your group experience.

5. Read the Outline of Each Session on the next pages so that you understand how the sessions will flow.

OUTLINE OF EACH SESSION

A TYPICAL GROUP SESSION FOR THE *HAND ME DOWNS* STUDY WILL INCLUDE THE FOLLOWING SECTIONS. READ THROUGH THIS TO GET A CLEAR IDEA OF HOW EACH GROUP MEETING WILL BE STRUCTURED.

WEEKLY MEMORY VERSE

Each session opens with a memory verse that emphasizes an important truth from the session. This is an optional exercise, but we believe that memorizing scripture can be a vital part of filling our minds with God's will for our lives. We encourage you to give this important habit a try. The verses for our six sessions are also listed in the appendix.

INTRODUCTION

Each lesson opens with a brief thought that will help you prepare for the session and get you thinking about the particular subject you will explore with your group. Make it a practice to read these before the session. You may want to have the group read them aloud.

SHARE YOUR STORY

The foundation for spiritual growth is an intimate connection with God's people. You build that connection by sharing your story with a few people who really know you and who earn your trust. This section includes some simple questions to get you talking—letting you share as much or as little of your story as you feel comfortable doing. Each session typically offers you two options. You can get to know your whole group by using the icebreaker question(s), or you can check in with one or two group members for a deeper connection and encouragement in your spiritual journey.

HEAR GOD'S STORY

In this section, you'll read the Bible and listen to teaching in order to hear God's story and begin to see how God's story aligns with yours. When the study directs you to, pop in the DVD and watch a short teaching segment. You'll then have an opportunity to read a passage of scripture and discuss both the teaching and the text. You won't focus on accumulating information but on how you should live in light of God's word. We help you apply the insights from scripture practically and creatively, from your heart as well as your head. At the end of the day, allowing the timeless truths from God's word to transform our lives in Christ should be your greatest aim.

CREATE A NEW STORY

God wants you to be a part of God's kingdom—to weave your story into the biblical story. That will mean change. It will require you to go God's way rather than your own. This won't happen overnight, but it should happen steadily. By making small, simple choices, we can begin to change our direction. This is where the Bible's instruction to "be doers of the word, and not only hearers" (James 1:22 CEB) come into play. Many people skip over this aspect of the Christian life because it's scary, relationally awkward, or simply too much work for their busy schedules. But Jesus wanted all of his disciples to know him personally, carry out his commands, and help outsiders connect with him. This doesn't necessarily mean preaching on street corners. It could mean hosting a short-term community group in your home, welcoming newcomers, or walking through this study with a friend. In this section, you'll have an opportunity to go beyond Bible study to actively doing Christian life together. This section will also have a question or two that will challenge you to live out your faith by serving others, sharing your faith, and worshipping God.

DIGGING DEEPER

If you have time and want to dig deeper into more Bible passages about the topic at hand, we've provided additional passages and questions, which you can use either during the meeting or as homework. Your group may choose to read and prepare before each meeting in order to cover more biblical material. Or group members can use the additional study section during the week after the meeting. If you prefer not to do homework, this section will provide you with plenty to discuss within the group. These options allow individuals or the whole group to expand their study while still accommodating those who can't do homework or are new to your group.

DAILY DEVOTIONS

Each week on the Daily Devotions pages, we provide scriptures to read between sessions—a month's worth of reflections to keep God's word near your heart. This provides you with a chance to slow down, read a small portion of scripture each day, and reflect and pray through it. You'll then have a chance to journal your response to what you've read and list the action steps God leads you to take. Use this section to seek God on your own throughout the week. This time at home should begin and end with prayer. Don't get in a hurry; take enough time to hear God's direction.

★ SESSION ONE ★

LEAVING A LEGACY

We won't hide them from their descendants; we'll tell the next generation all about the praise due the Lord.
Psalm 78:4 CEB

There's an old saying that "God doesn't have any grand-children." In other words, each one of us must make a decision for ourselves about whether we will follow and become God's adopted son or daughter. Just because our parents, family members, or friends are Christians doesn't mean we are. Our relationship with God isn't something we inherit from the generation before us—it's our choice.

However, the people close to us influence our lives and affect the way we think about our faith. God may not have grandchildren, but God often places grandparents, parents, and mentors in our lives who help us draw closer to Jesus. Perhaps some of these people modeled what it means to know Jesus. Or perhaps you're a "first generation" Christian. Whether you come from a long line of believers or you're the only one in your family, you belong to a spiritual family that needs your influence and example. Part of following Christ is leaving a legacy for others. Today we'll learn more about what it means to "hand down" our faith.

1

SHARE YOUR STORY

Each of us has a story. The events of our life—good, bad, wonderful, or challenging—shape who we are. God knows your story and intends to redeem it—to use every struggle and every joy to ultimately bring you into an accountable relationship with God. When we share our stories with others, we give them the opportunity to see God at work.

When we share our stories, we also realize we are not alone—that we have common experiences and thoughts, and others can understand what we are going through. Your story can encourage someone else. Telling it can lead to a path of freedom for you and for those you share it with.

Before you start this first meeting, get contact information for every participant. Take time to pass around a copy of the Community Group Roster on page 82, a sheet of paper, or your personal participant book, opened to the Comunity Group Roster. Ask someone to make copies or type up a list with everyone's information and e-mail it to the group during the week.

OPEN YOUR GROUP WITH PRAYER. THIS SHOULD BE A BRIEF, SIMPLE PRAYER IN WHICH YOU INVITE GOD TO GIVE YOU INSIGHT AS YOU STUDY. YOU CAN PRAY FOR SPECIFIC REQUESTS AT THE END OF THE MEETING, OR STOP MOMENTARILY TO PRAY IF A PARTICULAR SITUATION COMES UP DURING YOUR DISCUSSION.

Begin your time together by using the following questions and activities to get people talking.

- What brought you here? What do you hope to get out of this group?

- Were you raised in a Christian home? What role did faith, or religion, play in how you grew up?

- Whether your group is new or ongoing, it's always important to reflect on and review your values together. On page 80 is a Community Group Covenant with the values we've found most useful in sustaining healthy, balanced groups. We recommend that you choose one or two values—ones you haven't previously focused on or have room to grow in—to emphasize during this study. Choose ones that will take your group to the next stage of intimacy and spiritual health.

- We recommend you rotate host homes on a regular basis and let the hosts lead the meeting. Healthy groups rotate leadership. This helps to develop every member's ability to shepherd a few people in a safe environment. Even Jesus gave others the opportunity to serve alongside him (Mark 6:30-44). Look at the Frequent Questions in the appendicies for additional information about hosting or leading the group.

- The Community Group Calendar on page 81 is a tool for planning who will host and lead each meeting. Take a few minutes to select hosts and leaders for your remaining meetings. Don't skip this important step! It will revolutionize your group.

WATCH THE DVD

Use this space to record key thoughts, questions, and things you want to remember or follow up on. After watching the video, have someone read the discussion questions in the Hear God's Story section and direct the discussion among the group. As you go through each of the subsequent sections, ask someone else to read the questions and direct the discussion.

....

....

....

....

....

HEAR GOD'S STORY

READ 2 TIMOTHY 1:3-14

³I'M GRATEFUL TO GOD, WHOM I SERVE WITH A GOOD CONSCIENCE AS MY ANCESTORS DID. I CONSTANTLY REMEMBER YOU IN MY PRAYERS DAY AND NIGHT. ⁴WHEN I REMEMBER YOUR TEARS, I LONG TO SEE YOU SO THAT I CAN BE FILLED WITH HAPPINESS. ⁵I'M REMINDED OF YOUR AUTHENTIC FAITH, WHICH FIRST LIVED IN YOUR GRANDMOTHER LOIS AND YOUR MOTHER EUNICE. I'M SURE THAT THIS FAITH IS ALSO INSIDE YOU. ⁶BECAUSE OF THIS, I'M REMINDING YOU TO REVIVE GOD'S GIFT THAT IS IN YOU THROUGH THE LAYING ON OF MY HANDS. ⁷GOD DIDN'T GIVE US A SPIRIT THAT IS TIMID BUT ONE THAT IS POWERFUL, LOVING, AND SELF-CONTROLLED.

⁸SO DON'T BE ASHAMED OF THE TESTIMONY ABOUT THE LORD OR OF ME, HIS PRISONER. INSTEAD, SHARE THE SUFFERING FOR THE GOOD NEWS, DEPENDING ON GOD'S POWER. ⁹GOD IS THE ONE WHO SAVED AND CALLED US WITH A HOLY CALLING. THIS WASN'T BASED ON WHAT WE HAVE DONE, BUT IT WAS BASED ON HIS OWN PURPOSE AND GRACE THAT HE GAVE US IN CHRIST JESUS BEFORE TIME BEGAN. ¹⁰NOW HIS GRACE IS REVEALED THROUGH THE APPEARANCE OF OUR SAVIOR, CHRIST JESUS. HE DESTROYED DEATH AND BROUGHT LIFE AND IMMORTALITY INTO CLEAR FOCUS THROUGH THE GOOD NEWS. ¹¹I WAS APPOINTED A MESSENGER, APOSTLE, AND TEACHER OF THIS GOOD NEWS. ¹²THIS IS ALSO WHY I'M SUFFERING THE WAY I DO, BUT I'M NOT ASHAMED. I KNOW THE ONE IN WHOM I'VE PLACED MY TRUST. I'M CONVINCED THAT GOD IS POWERFUL ENOUGH TO PROTECT WHAT HE HAS PLACED IN MY TRUST UNTIL THAT DAY. ¹³HOLD ON TO THE PATTERN OF SOUND TEACHING THAT YOU HEARD FROM ME WITH THE FAITH AND LOVE THAT ARE IN CHRIST JESUS. ¹⁴PROTECT THIS GOOD THING THAT HAS BEEN PLACED IN YOUR TRUST THROUGH THE HOLY SPIRIT WHO LIVES IN US. (CEB)

1. Who has poured into your life the way Lois, Eunice, and Paul poured into Timothy's life?

2. In verse 6, Timothy is encouraged to revive the gifts of God within him. How might he, and we, rekindle our gifts?

3. Paul encourages Timothy to guard or protect the good thing he received. How might he have done that when Christians were harassed for living faithfully and worshipping God?

CREATE A
NEW STORY

GOD INVITES YOU TO BE PART OF THE KINGDOM—TO WEAVE YOUR STORY INTO GOD'S. THAT WILL MEAN CHANGE—TO GO GOD'S WAY RATHER THAN YOUR OWN. THIS WON'T HAPPEN OVERNIGHT, BUT IT SHOULD HAPPEN STEADILY. BY STARTING WITH SMALL, SIMPLE CHOICES, WE BEGIN TO CHANGE OUR DIRECTION. THE HOLY SPIRIT HELPS US ALONG THE WAY— GIVING US GIFTS TO SERVE THE BODY, OFFERING US INSIGHTS INTO SCRIPTURE, AND CHALLENGING US TO LOVE NOT ONLY THOSE AROUND US BUT THOSE FAR FROM GOD.

TAKE A LOOK AT THE SEGMENTS BELOW, AND WRITE THE NAMES OF TWO OR THREE PEOPLE YOU KNOW WHO NEED TO KNOW CHRIST. COMMIT TO PRAYING FOR GOD'S GUIDANCE AND AN OPPORTUNITY TO SHARE WITH EACH OF THEM. PERHAPS THEY WOULD BE OPEN TO JOINING THE GROUP? SHARE YOUR LISTS WITH THE GROUP SO YOU CAN ALL BE PRAYING FOR THE PEOPLE YOU'VE IDENTIFIED.

FAMILY (immediate or extended)	
FAMILIAR (neighbors, kids' sports teams, school, and so forth)	
FRIENDS	
FUN (gym, hobbies, hangouts)	
FIRM (work)	

IN THIS SECTION, TALK ABOUT HOW YOU WILL APPLY THE WISDOM YOU'VE LEARNED FROM THE TEACHING AND BIBLE STUDY. THEN THINK ABOUT PRACTICAL STEPS YOU CAN TAKE IN THE COMING WEEK TO LIVE OUT WHAT YOU'VE LEARNED.

1. What is one positive hand-me-down that you are passing on to those around you?

2. What is one aspect of your legacy that you would like to change? How can this group help you do that?

3. When people consider your legacy, what would you like them to say?

4. This week, how will you interact with the Bible? Can you commit to spending time in daily prayer or study of God's word? Use the Daily Devotions section to guide you. Tell the group how you plan to follow Jesus this week, and then, at your next meeting, talk about your progress and challenges.

5. Stack your hands just like a sports team does in the huddle, and commit to taking a risk and going deeper in your group and in your relationships with each other.

6. To close your time together, spend some time worshipping God together—praying, singing, and/or reading scripture.

> Consider someone–in this group or outside it–who you can begin going deeper with in an intentional way. This might be your mom or dad, a cousin, an aunt or uncle, a roommate, a college buddy, or a neighbor. Choose someone who might be open to "doing life" with you at a deeper level and pray about that opportunity.

- Have someone use his or her musical gifts to lead the group in a worship song. Try singing a capella, using a worship CD, or having someone accompany your singing with a musical instrument.

- Choose a psalm or other favorite verse and read it aloud together. Make it a time of praise and worship as the words remind you of all God has done for you.

- Ask, "How can we pray for you this week?" Invite everyone to share, but don't force the issue. Be sure to write prayer requests on your Prayer Requests and Praise Reports sheet on page 85.

- Close your meeting with prayer.

If you feel God nudging you to go deeper, take some time before the next meeting to dig into God's word. Explore these Bible passages related to this session's theme on your own and jot your reflections in a journal or in this study guide. A great way to gain insight on a passage is to read it in several different translations. You may even want to use a Bible website or app to look up commentary on these passages.

Read Psalm 78:1-8

[1]Listen, my people, to my teaching; tilt your ears toward the words of my mouth. [2]I will open my mouth with a proverb. I'll declare riddles from days long gone—[3]ones that we've heard and learned about, ones that our ancestors told us. [4]We won't hide them from their descendants; we'll tell the next generation all about the praise due the Lord and his strength—the wondrous works God has done. [5]He established a law for Jacob and set up Instruction for Israel, ordering our ancestors to teach them to their children. [6]This is so that the next generation and children not yet born will know these things, and so they can rise up and tell their children [7]to put their hope in God—never forgetting God's deeds, but keeping God's commandments—[8]and so that they won't become like their ancestors: a rebellious, stubborn generation, a generation whose heart wasn't set firm and whose spirit wasn't faithful to God. (CEB)

1. Why is it so important to talk about our heritage with our kids?

2. How can we share God with the next generation?

3. What are the implications of this scripture for your country, family, and life?

Read Joshua 24:14-18

¹⁴"So now, revere the Lord. Serve him honestly and faithfully. Put aside the gods that your ancestors served beyond the Euphrates and in Egypt and serve the Lord. ¹⁵But if it seems wrong in your opinion to serve the Lord, then choose today whom you will serve. Choose the gods whom your ancestors served beyond the Euphrates or the gods of the Amorites in whose land you live. But my family and I will serve the Lord."

¹⁶Then the people answered, "God forbid that we ever leave the Lord to serve other gods! ¹⁷The Lord is our God. He is the one who brought us and our ancestors up from the land of Egypt, from the house of bondage. He has done these mighty signs in our sight. He has protected us the whole way we've gone and in all the nations through which we've passed. ¹⁸The Lord has driven out all the nations before us, including the Amorites who lived in the land. We too will serve the Lord, because he is our God." (CEB)

1. What does it mean to fear God?

2. What word appears the most in verses 14 and 15? What does this tell you about one way we can build our families and leave a legacy?

3. How does Joshua's example with his own family encourage the people? What is their response?

DAILY DEVOTIONS

Day 1 • Read Deuteronomy 6:6-7

These words that I am commanding you today must always be on your minds. Recite them to your children. Talk about them when you are sitting around your house and when you are out and about, when you are lying down and when you are getting up. (CEB)

Respond:

How can you keep God's commandments on your heart? What are some ways to impress them on your children?

My Action Steps: ....

Day 2 • Read 2 Timothy 2:2

Take the things you heard me say in front of many other witnesses and pass them on to faithful people who are also capable of teaching others. (CEB)

Respond:

Our legacy is not limited to our families. How can you share your wisdom with friends or colleagues who can continue your work when you're gone?

My Action Steps: ....

Day 3 • Read Joshua 4:6-7

In the future your children may ask, "What do these stones mean to you?" Then you will tell them that the water of the Jordan was cut off before the LORD's covenant chest. When it crossed over the Jordan, the water of the Jordan was cut off. These stones will be an enduring memorial for the Israelites. (CEB)

Respond:

Several times in scripture, God instructs the people to use tangible objects as symbols of God's faithfulness and as "teaching points" for future generations. How might you apply this idea to your own family?

My Action Steps: ....

Day 4 • Read Psalm 103:17-18

But the LORD's faithful love is from forever ago to forever from now for those who honor him. And God's righteousness reaches to the grandchildren of those who keep his covenant and remember to keep his commands. (CEB)

Respond:

What does the last sentence say we should do if we want the Lord to reach future generations? How does this contribute to our "grandchildren" knowing God?

My Action Steps: ....

Day 5 • Read 1 Corinthians 15:3-5

I passed on to you as most important what I also received:
Christ died for our sins in line with the scriptures, he was bur-
ied, and he rose on the third day in line with the scriptures. He
appeared to Cephas, then to the Twelve. (CEB)

Respond:

Paul both received the faith and passed it on, emphasizing
its importance. Who needs to receive the faith you have to
share? Ask God to give you opportunities to pass it on.

My Action Steps: ....

Day 6

Use the following space to write any thoughts God has put in
your heart and mind about the things we have looked at in
this session and during your Daily Devotions time this week.

....

....

....

....

....

MODELING HOLY HABITS

TRAIN YOURSELF FOR A HOLY LIFE!
1 TIMOTHY 4:7 CEB

Nature or nurture? It's an ongoing debate. Some things we're born with—the color of our hair, the way we laugh, whether we're more outgoing or more shy. Other things are the result of what we experience and how we're raised. A baby born in France will learn French, while a child growing up in Spain will speak Spanish.

Scientists debate whether nature or nurture is most important, but almost all of them agree both are significant. You were born with unique personality traits and characteristics, and you've also been molded and shaped by your life and by the people in it.

This is great news when it comes to our own roles as parents, friends, and family members. While we can't change another person's basic nature, we can have a huge impact on his or her nurture. In fact, God's word tells us we're called to do just that! From the words we say to the things we do, our choices can model what it looks like to have a relationship with Jesus. Today we'll take a closer look at the huge privilege and responsibility we have to "nurture" other people through our example.

SHARE
YOUR
STORY

As we said last week, when we share our stories with others, we give them the opportunity to see God at work. Even in this moment, your story is being shaped by being a part of this group. In fact, few things can shape us more than community.

Open your group with prayer. This should be a brief, simple prayer, in which you invite God to be with you as you meet. You can pray for specific requests at the end of the meeting or stop momentarily to pray if a particular situation comes up during your discussion.

Begin your time together by using the following questions and activities to get people talking:

1. What is one genetic trait (eye color, hair texture, height, strength, athletic ability, etc.) that was passed on to you that you like?

2. What is a hand-me-down, genetic or environmental, that you would rather not have?

> **W**HEN WE SHARE OUR STORIES, WE CAN ENCOURAGE SOMEONE ELSE AND LEARN. **A**S **G**OD HELPS US BE BRAVE ENOUGH TO REVEAL OUR THOUGHTS AND FEELINGS, WE EXPERIENCE THE PRESENCE OF **G**OD.

3. When has a bad habit gotten you into trouble?

WATCH
THE
DVD

WATCH THE DVD FOR THIS SESSION NOW. USE THE SPACE PROVIDED TO RECORD KEY THOUGHTS, QUESTIONS, AND THINGS YOU WANT TO REMEMBER OR FOLLOW UP ON. AFTER THE VIDEO, HAVE SOMEONE READ THE DISCUSSION QUESTIONS IN THE HEAR GOD'S STORY SECTION AND DIRECT THE DISCUSSION AMONG THE GROUP. AS YOU GO THROUGH EACH OF THE SUBSEQUENT SECTIONS, ASK SOMEONE ELSE TO READ THE QUESTIONS AND DIRECT THE DISCUSSION.

HEAR GOD'S STORY

After viewing the DVD, use the following questions to guide your discussion of the teaching from the video.

READ 1 TIMOTHY 4:7-9

7But stay away from the godless myths that are passed down from the older women. Train yourself for a holy life! 8While physical training has some value, training in holy living is useful for everything. It has promise for this life now and the life to come. 9This saying is reliable and deserves complete acceptance. (CEB)

1. What myths or tales might these early Christians have been influenced by?

2. How do we train ourselves to be godly?

3. How is spiritual training superior to physical training?

4. What value does godliness have in this life? In the life to come?

CREATE A
NEW STORY

God invites you to be part of the kingdom—to weave your story into God's. That will mean change—to go God's way rather than your own. This won't happen overnight, but it should happen steadily. By starting with small, simple choices, we begin to change our direction. The Holy Spirit helps us along the way—giving us gifts to serve the body, offering us insights into Scripture, and challenging us to love not only those around us but those far from God.

CREATE A NEW STORY

1. Of the four habits Jen mentions—spending time in God's word, spending time in prayer, honoring God through giving, and gathering with other believers—which one is easiest for you? Which one is most difficult?

2. Why is it so important that we spend time with other Christians? How does that connect to this week's idea of modeling spiritual growth?

3. Do you have a story about how any or all of these habits have helped you during a tough time? If so, consider sharing it with the group.

4. Many of these habits are personal; they're things we often do on our own. How can we appropriately include others in these habits, especially our children?

5. Are you wholeheartedly passing on your faith? If not, what's standing in your way?

6. Here are some simple ways to connect with God. Tell the group which ones you plan to try this week, and talk about your progress and challenges when you meet next time.

- ## PRAYER
  Commit to personal prayer and daily connection with God. You may find it helpful to write your prayers in a journal.

- ## DAILY DEVOTIONS
  The Daily Devotions provided in each session offer an opportunity to read a short Bible passage five days a week during the course of our study. In our hurry-up world, we often move too quickly through everything—even reading God's word! Slow down. Don't just skim, but take time to read carefully and reflect on the passage. Write down your insights on what you read each day. Copy a portion of scripture on a card and tape it somewhere in your line of sight, such as your car's dashboard or the bathroom mirror. Or text it to yourself! Think about it when you sit at red lights or while you're eating a meal. Reflect on what God is saying to you through these words. On the sixth day summarize what God has shown you throughout the week.

7. To close your time together, spend some time worshipping God together: praying, singing, and/or reading scripture.

- Have someone use his or her musical gifts to lead the group in a worship song. Try singing a capella, using a worship CD, or having someone accompany your singing with a musical instrument.

- Choose a psalm or other favorite verse and read it aloud together. Make it a time of praise and worship, as the words remind you of all God has done for you.

- Ask, "How can we pray for you this week?" Invite everyone to share, but don't force the issue. Be sure to write prayer requests on your Prayer Requests and Praise Reports sheet on page 85.

- Close your meeting with prayer.

DIGGING DEEPER

IF YOU FEEL GOD IS NUDGING YOU TO GO DEEPER, TAKE SOME TIME BETWEEN NOW AND OUR NEXT MEETING TO DIG INTO GOD'S WORD. EXPLORE THE BIBLE PASSAGES RELATED TO THIS SESSION'S THEME ON YOUR OWN, JOTTING YOUR REFLECTIONS IN A JOURNAL OR IN THIS PARTICIPANT BOOK. WANT TO GO DEEPER? SELECT A FEW VERSES AND TRY PARAPHRASING THEM—WRITING THEM IN YOUR OWN WORDS. IF YOU LIKE, SHARE THEM WITH THE GROUP THE NEXT TIME YOU MEET.

Read 1 Timothy 4:7-9

⁷But stay away from the godless myths that are passed down from the older women. Train yourself for a holy life! ⁸While physical training has some value, training in holy living is useful for everything. It has promise for this life now and the life to come. ⁹This saying is reliable and deserves complete acceptance. (CEB)

1. In verse 7, Paul seems to be saying we shouldn't focus on things that distract us from God. What are some of those things in your life?

2. What are some ways we train ourselves to be more physically fit? How might we make ourselves more spiritually fit?

3. How is spiritual training more important than physical training?

4. How does becoming more like Jesus improve our lives now? What makes it a goal worth pursuing?

DAILY DEVOTIONS

Day 1 • Read Proverbs 27:17

As iron sharpens iron, so friends sharpen each other's faces. (CEB)

Respond:

How do people "sharpen" one another? Who is playing this role in your life? Are you sharpening anyone else?

My Action Steps: ....

Day 2 • Read 1 Peter 3:8

Finally, all of you be of one mind, sympathetic, lovers of your fellow believers, compassionate, and modest in your opinion of yourselves. (CEB)

Respond:

Which of these actions do you find easiest when it comes to relationships with others? How does living this way help you share your faith with those close to you?

My Action Steps: ....

Day 3 • Read 2 Timothy 4:2

Preach the word. Be ready to do it whether it is convenient or inconvenient. Correct, confront, and encourage with patience and instruction. (CEB)

Respond:

This verse was written from one preacher (Paul) to another (Timothy), but it applies to any of us wanting to model a lifestyle of faith. Take a few moments to ask God for help in following this instruction.

My Action Steps: ....

Day 4 • Read Proverbs 22:6

Train a child in the way they should go; when they grow old, they won't depart from it. (CEB)

Respond:

Of course, there are no guarantees in life—we all know people who raised their children well and the children did, in fact, "depart from it." But the Proverbs share wisdom that is generally true for living a good life. Does this verse give you hope? How can you grow in the way you are training your child?

My Action Steps: ....

Day 5 • Read 1 John 4:11-12

Dear friends, if God loved us this way, we also ought to love each other. No one has ever seen God. If we love each other, God remains in us and his love is made perfect in us. (CEB)

Respond:

You might be one of the biggest ways someone else sees God. It's a huge responsibility but also a huge opportunity. How can you show God and God's love to the people in your life today?

My Action Steps: ....

Day 6

Use the following space to write any thoughts God has put in your heart and mind about the things we have looked at in this session and during your Daily Devotions time this week.

....

....

....

....

....

....

BREAKING BAD CYCLES

WE MUST SEARCH AND EXAMINE OUR WAYS; WE MUST
RETURN TO THE LORD.
LAMENTATIONS 3:40 CEB

Some of us grew up wearing a lot of hand-me-downs. Perhaps these used clothes came from an older brother or sister who outgrew them, or maybe your mom swapped clothes with other moms who had kids your age. One of our friends regularly received bags of clothes from another girl at church who was three years older, and she said it was like Christmas—there was always at least one great find in each bag.

On the other hand, anyone who's received hand-me-downs knows there are also items you just don't want: the pants two sizes too small, the shirt with a band name on it that isn't popular anymore, the winter hat that you hated wearing. Just because someone wanted to give you something doesn't mean you always wanted to receive it.

The same is true with the values, attitudes, and beliefs that are handed down to us. As we've discussed the last two weeks, our family and friends may have gifted us with an amazing spiritual legacy. But we've probably also inherited some negative patterns and destructive habits. Today we'll talk about how to discern what we should keep and what needs to go, and how we can create new patterns that honor God.

SHARE
YOUR
STORY

Open your group with prayer. This should be a brief, simple prayer in which you invite God to be with you as you meet. You can pray for specific requests at the end of the meeting, or stop momentarily to pray if a particular situation comes up during your discussion.

Sharing personal stories builds deeper connections among group members. Begin your time together by using the following questions and activities to get people talking.

1. Did you get many hand-me-down clothes as a kid? Did you hate it or enjoy it?

2. What's the hardest habit you've ever tried to break?

3. What's a habit you wish was part of your life?

WATCH
THE
DVD

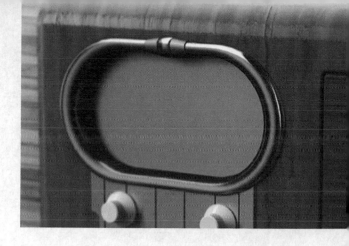

WATCH THE DVD FOR THIS SESSION NOW. USE THIS SPACE TO
RECORD KEY THOUGHTS, QUESTIONS, AND THINGS YOU WANT TO
REMEMBER OR FOLLOW UP ON.

....

....

....

....

....

HEAR GOD'S STORY

AFTER VIEWING THE DVD, USE THE FOLLOWING QUESTIONS TO GUIDE YOUR DISCUSSION OF THE TEACHING FROM THE VIDEO.

READ 2 CHRONICLES 34:3-5

³IN THE EIGHTH YEAR OF HIS [JOSIAH'S] RULE, WHILE HE WAS JUST A BOY, HE BEGAN TO SEEK THE GOD OF HIS ANCESTOR DAVID, AND IN THE TWELFTH YEAR HE BEGAN PURIFYING JUDAH AND JERUSALEM OF THE SHRINES, THE SACRED POLES, IDOLS, AND IMAGES. ⁴UNDER HIS SUPERVISION, THE ALTARS FOR THE BAALS WERE TORN DOWN, AND THE INCENSE ALTARS THAT WERE ABOVE THEM WERE SMASHED. HE BROKE UP THE SACRED POLES, IDOLS, AND IMAGES, GRINDING THEM TO DUST AND SCATTERING THEM OVER THE GRAVES OF THOSE WHO HAD SACRIFICED TO THEM. ⁵HE BURNED THE BONES OF THE PRIESTS ON THEIR ALTARS, PURIFYING JUDAH AND JERUSALEM. (CEB)

1. What are some ways you've successfully formed a new habit or added a new priority to your life?

2. What's something that was the "norm" in your household growing up that you now recognize was not so great? Have you carried on those patterns into your life today?

3. King Josiah inherited a huge spiritual mess from his father and grandfather. What does their story teach us about cleaning up the messes we have inherited? How does it encourage you?

4. What does it mean to seek after God like Josiah did? How would your life change if you began seeking God more intentionally?

5. Finding the scriptures gave Josiah the knowledge of what God expected and how the kingdom needed to change. How can spending time reading God's word give insight into your own life?

CREATE A NEW STORY

God invites you to be part of the kingdom—to weave your story into God's story. That will mean change. It will require you to go God's way rather than your own. This won't happen overnight, but it should happen steadily. By making small, simple choices, we can begin to change our direction. The Holy Spirit helps us along the way, by giving us gifts to serve the body, offering us insights into scripture, and challenging us to love not only those around us but those far from God.

IN THIS SECTION, TALK ABOUT HOW YOU WILL APPLY THE WISDOM YOU'VE LEARNED IN THIS SESSION.

1. In the video Jim said, "Part of leaving a faithful legacy is examining your life and breaking negative cycles." What cycles do you need to break?

2. What are some positive patterns you want to be sure to pass on to others? What are some practical steps you can take to begin creating these new habits?

3. How do our habits contribute to our legacy?

4. Groups grow closer when they serve together. How could your group serve someone in need? You may want to visit a shut-in from your church, provide a meal for a family who is going through a difficult time, or give some other practical help. If nothing comes to mind, spend some group time praying and asking God to show you who needs your help. Then have two or three group members organize a service project for the group, and do it!

5. Developing our ability to serve according to the leading of the Holy Spirit takes time and persistence in getting to know our Lord. So the first step toward serving others is, paradoxically, spending time alone with God—praying and studying and reflecting on God's word. What specific steps will you take this week? If you've focused on prayer in past weeks, maybe you'll want to direct your attention to scripture this week. If you've been reading God's word consistently, perhaps you'll want to take it deeper and try memorizing a verse. Tell the group what you plan to try this week, and talk about your progress and challenges when you meet next time.

6. To close your time together, spend some time worshipping God together—praying, singing, and/or reading scripture.

- Have someone use his or her musical gifts to lead the group in a worship song. Try singing a capella, using a worship CD, or having someone accompany your singing with a musical instrument.

- Choose a psalm or other favorite verse and read it aloud together. Make it a time of praise and worship, as the words remind you of all God has done for you.

- Ask, "How can we pray for you this week?" Invite everyone to share, but don't force the issue. Be sure to write prayer requests on your Prayer Requests and Praise Reports sheet on page 85.

- Close your meeting with prayer.

TAKE SOME TIME BETWEEN NOW
AND OUR NEXT MEETING TO DIG
INTO GOD'S WORD. EXPLORE THE
BIBLE PASSAGES RELATED TO THIS
SESSION'S THEME. JOT DOWN YOUR
REFLECTIONS IN A JOURNAL OR IN
THIS STUDY GUIDE. YOU MAY EVEN
WANT TO USE A BIBLE WEBSITE
OR APP TO LOOK UP COMMENTARY
ON THESE PASSAGES. IF YOU LIKE,
SHARE WHAT YOU LEARN WITH THE
GROUP THE NEXT TIME YOU MEET.

DIGGING DEEPER

Read Hebrews 12:1-3

¹So then let's also run the race that is laid out in front of us, since we have such a great cloud of witnesses surrounding us. Let's throw off any extra baggage, get rid of the sin that trips us up, ²and fix our eyes on Jesus, faith's pioneer and perfecter. He endured the cross, ignoring the shame, for the sake of the joy that was laid out in front of him, and sat down at the right side of God's throne.
³Think about the one who endured such opposition from sinners so that you won't be discouraged and you won't give up. (CEB)

1. How does being surrounded by witnesses make you feel?

2. What sins have often hindered or entangled you?

3. How would your life change if you began to live for an audience of one—God?

Read Ephesians 4:22-24

²²Change the former way of life that was part of the person you once were, corrupted by deceitful desires. ²³Instead, renew the thinking in your mind by the Spirit ²⁴and clothe yourself with the new person created according to God's image in justice and true holiness. (CEB)

1. What is one thing you've been taught by a pastor, Bible reading, or a spiritual mentor that you need to incorporate into your life?

2. How can desires deceive us? How do they corrupt us?

3. How do our attitudes affect our spiritual growth?

4. What a great thing it is to know we were created to be like God! How does knowing God's plan for you give you hope in following God?

DAILY DEVOTIONS

Day 1 • Read Romans 12:21

Don't be defeated by evil, but defeat evil with good. (CEB)

Respond:

How can we live out this verse in our daily lives? Ask God for insight and for help in how you can overcome the bad in your life and replace it with good.

My Action Steps: ....

Day 2 • Read 1 Corinthians 10:13

No temptation has seized you that isn't common for people. But God is faithful. He won't allow you to be tempted beyond your abilities. Instead, with the temptation, God will also supply a way out so that you will be able to endure it. (CEB)

Respond:

Does this verse encourage you or discourage you? How does God provide ways out of our temptations?

My Action Steps: ....

Day 3 • Read 1 John 1:9

But if we confess our sins, he is faithful and just to forgive us our sins and cleanse us from everything we've done wrong. (CEB)

Respond:

Confessing our sin and then accepting God's forgiveness is key to breaking negative cycles. Take a few minutes to admit your mistakes to God, and then rest in the knowledge that you are forgiven.

My Action Steps: ....

Day 4 • Read 1 John 2:17

And the world and its cravings are passing away, but the person who does the will of God remains forever. (CEB)

Respond:

What are the desires of the world? How are they different from the will of God?

My Action Steps: ....

Day 5 • Read James 1:12

Those who stand firm during testing are blessed. They are tried and true. They will receive the life God has promised to those who love him as their reward. (CEB)

Respond:

If you are struggling to change negative patterns and receiving resistance from other people, ask God to help you persevere in following God. Spend a few minutes meditating on this passage and thanking God for the blessings God promises.

My Action Steps: ....

....

Day 6

Use the following space to write any thoughts God has put in your heart and mind about the things we have looked at in this session and during your Daily Devotions time this week.

....

....

....

....

....

....

★ SESSION FOUR ★

LIVING WITH INTEGRITY

THE RIGHTEOUS LIVE WITH INTEGRITY;
HAPPY ARE THEIR CHILDREN WHO COME AFTER THEM.
PROVERBS 20:7 CEB

Researchers at Northwestern University ran a series of experiments that placed college students in tempting situations to smoke, eat junk food, or avoid studying. They found we often display what's called a *restraint bias*, which means we tend to overestimate how much self-control we will have against temptation. In other words, we're biased to think we have more restraint than we do. When we're not in the situation, we think we'll handle it great, but in the heat of the moment we'll often give in.

This isn't such a big deal if it means we eat a little more pizza than we should or we go to bed a little later than we intend to. But sometimes we have a restraint bias when it comes to more serious things. We not only lack willpower, we also lack self-awareness. We think we can easily handle a difficult situation. We assume that our good intentions will stay a reality when things get tough, and we generally overestimate our ability to do the right thing.

We can't live moral lives and please God through our willpower. If we try, we'll fail again and again. But we can please God when we follow Christ and allow God to work in us. This week we'll learn more about what it means to live with integrity—not through our own strength but through God's.

SHARE
YOUR
STORY

Open your group with prayer. This should be a brief, simple prayer in which you invite God to be with you as you meet. You can pray for specific requests at the end of the meeting or stop momentarily to pray if a particular situation comes up during your discussion.

As we have said in previous lessons, sharing our personal stories builds deeper connections among group members. Your story may be exactly what another person needs to hear to encourage or strengthen them. And your listening to others' stories is an act of love and kindness to them—and could very well help them to grow spiritually. Begin your time together by using the following questions and activities to get people talking.

1. When you think of someone with strong integrity who comes to mind? How does he or she influence you?

2. What character values (work ethic, honesty, responsibility, fairness, kindness, generosity, etc.) had a strong emphasis in your home growing up?

3. You may want to sit and share with your spiritual partners your prayer concerns.

WATCH
THE
DVD

WATCH THE DVD FOR THIS SESSION NOW. USE THIS SPACE TO RECORD KEY THOUGHTS, QUESTIONS, AND THINGS YOU WANT TO REMEMBER OR FOLLOW UP ON. AFTER YOU FINISH WATCHING THE VIDEO, HAVE SOMEONE READ THE DISCUSSION QUESTIONS IN THE HEAR GOD'S STORY SECTION AND DIRECT THE DISCUSSION AMONG THE GROUP. AS YOU GO THROUGH EACH OF THE SUBSEQUENT SECTIONS, ASK SOMEONE ELSE TO READ THE QUESTIONS AND DIRECT THE DISCUSSION.

HEAR GOD'S STORY

USE THE FOLLOWING QUESTIONS TO GUIDE YOUR DISCUSSION OF THE TEACHING FROM THE VIDEO AND THE BIBLE PASSAGE BELOW.

READ 2 CORINTHIANS 5:21
GOD CAUSED THE ONE WHO DIDN'T KNOW SIN TO BE SIN FOR OUR SAKE SO THAT THROUGH HIM WE COULD BECOME THE RIGHTEOUSNESS OF GOD. (CEB)

1. What does it mean for values to be "caught" instead of "taught"?

2. In what areas do you currently "own" integrity? In what ways do you need to work on building integrity?

3. What's wrong with trying to develop integrity or become a better person by yourself?

4. What's God's part in you growing as a person? What's your part?

CREATE A NEW STORY

GOD INVITES YOU TO BE PART OF THE KINGDOM—TO WEAVE YOUR STORY INTO GOD'S STORY. THAT WILL MEAN CHANGE. IT WILL REQUIRE YOU TO GO GOD'S WAY RATHER THAN YOUR OWN. THIS WON'T HAPPEN OVERNIGHT, BUT IT SHOULD HAPPEN STEADILY. BY MAKING SMALL, SIMPLE CHOICES, WE CAN BEGIN TO CHANGE OUR DIRECTION. THE HOLY SPIRIT HELPS US ALONG THE WAY—GIVING US GIFTS TO SERVE THE BODY, OFFERING US INSIGHTS INTO SCRIPTURE, AND CHALLENGING US TO LOVE NOT ONLY THOSE AROUND US BUT THOSE FAR FROM GOD.

1. What areas of your integrity are strong? Which areas need work?

2. What are some values you have been taught by others? What are some values you've "caught"?

3. What are the key values you'd like your family or friends to learn from you? How can you be more intentional about handing them out?

4. Do you need to do your part and follow the ABC steps Jim mentioned in the DVD?

5. Spend some time praying about those you know who might respond to a simple invitation: to come to a church service, to join your small group, or even just to have coffee and talk about spiritual matters. Ask the Holy Spirit to bring to mind people you can pray for.

DIGGING DEEPER

Read 1 Peter 2:23-25

23When he was insulted, he did not reply with insults. When he suffered, he did not threaten revenge. Instead, he entrusted himself to the one who judges justly. 24He carried in his own body on the cross the sins we committed. He did this so that we might live in righteousness, having nothing to do with sin. By his wounds you were healed. 25Though you were like straying sheep, you have now returned to the shepherd and guardian of your lives. (CEB)

1. How did Jesus entrust himself to God on the cross?

2. What does it mean to die to sins? To live for righteousness?

3. How is Jesus a shepherd to us?

Read 1 John 4:9-12

9This is how the love of God is revealed to us: God has sent his only Son into the world so that we can live through him. 10This is love: it is not that we loved God but that he loved us and sent his Son as the sacrifice that deals with our sins.

11Dear friends, if God loved us this way, we also ought to love each other. 12No one has ever seen God. If we love each other, God remains in us and his love is made perfect in us. (CEB)

1. What does it mean to live through God's son?

2. How does Jesus's sacrifice reconcile us with God for our sin?

3. How does God's love live in us when we love each other?

DAILY DEVOTIONS

Day 1 • Read Isaiah 53:5

He was pierced because of our rebellions and crushed because of our crimes. He bore the punishment that made us whole; by his wounds we are healed. (CEB)

Respond:

How does Jesus's "punishment" bring us peace? How do his physical wounds bring us spiritual healing?

My Action Steps: ....

Day 2 • Read Colossians 1:13-14

He rescued us from the control of darkness and transferred us into the kingdom of the Son he loves. He set us free through the Son and forgave our sins. (CEB)

Respond:

How do you respond to the idea of being rescued? Have you ever considered the idea of needing to be rescued from your sins?

My Action Steps: ....

Day 3 • Read Ephesians 5:1-2

Therefore, imitate God like dearly loved children. Live your life with love, following the example of Christ, who loved us and gave himself for us. He was a sacrificial offering that smelled sweet to God. (CEB)

Respond:

What does it mean that Jesus "smelled sweet"? Ask for his help today to walk in the way of love.

My Action Steps: ....

Day 4 • Read Romans 8:1-2

So now there isn't any condemnation for those who are in Christ Jesus. The law of the Spirit of life in Christ Jesus has set you free from the law of sin and death. (CEB)

Respond:

As we try to follow God and live with more integrity, we can take comfort in knowing that God is not angry if we fail. We have the freedom to grow and even make mistakes because we are in Christ.

My Action Steps: ....

Day 5 • Read John 15:13

No one has greater love than to give up one's life for one's friends. (CEB)

Respond:

Take some time today simply to thank Jesus for dying for your sins and to ask for his help in becoming a person of integrity.

My Action Steps: ....

Day 6

Use the following space to write any thoughts God has put in your heart and mind about the things we have looked at in this session and during your Daily Devotions time this week.

....

....

....

....

....

....

PLAYING WELL WITH OTHERS

IF POSSIBLE, TO THE BEST OF YOUR ABILITY,
LIVE AT PEACE WITH ALL PEOPLE.
ROMANS 12:18 CEB

Have you ever known a really mean Christian? Unfortunately, there are some out there. As we've talked about in this study, we are all deeply affected by the attitudes, habits, and values of others, and sometimes these can leave lasting scars that cause a person to hurt deeply—and to hurt others.

But as Christ followers, our behavior not only reflects on us, it also reflects on Jesus. Part of loving God is loving other people. Part of becoming like Christ is learning to love like he did. We'll never get it perfect, but the Bible is full of instructions for how we are to consistently work toward loving, serving, and honoring the people in our lives. Sometimes this is easy, like offering a smile to a stranger. Sometimes it's more difficult, like offering forgiveness. But no matter what each day holds, God's teaching is clear—we need to learn how to play well with others. Let's dive in and learn more about what that means.

SHARE YOUR STORY

1. Without naming names, who's the most difficult person in your life?

2. What's your "go-to" when you're angry, stressed, or unhappy? For instance, do you shut down and get quiet? Do you yell? Do you get sarcastic?

WATCH
THE
DVD

WATCH THE DVD FOR THIS SESSION NOW. USE THIS SPACE TO RECORD KEY THOUGHTS, QUESTIONS, AND THINGS YOU WANT TO REMEMBER OR FOLLOW UP ON. AFTER YOU FINISH WATCHING THE VIDEO, HAVE SOMEONE READ THE DISCUSSION QUESTIONS IN THE HEAR GOD'S STORY SECTION AND DIRECT THE DISCUSSION AMONG THE GROUP. AS YOU GO THROUGH EACH OF THE SUBSEQUENT SECTIONS, ASK SOMEONE ELSE TO READ THE QUESTIONS AND DIRECT THE DISCUSSION.

HEAR GOD'S STORY

After viewing the DVD Session, use the following questions to guide your discussion of the teaching from the video and this Bible passage from Romans.

READ ROMANS 12:9-18

[9]Love should be shown without pretending. Hate evil, and hold on to what is good. [10]Love each other like the members of your family. Be the best at showing honor to each other. [11]Don't hesitate to be enthusiastic—be on fire in the Spirit as you serve the Lord! [12]Be happy in your hope, stand your ground when you're in trouble, and devote yourselves to prayer. [13]Contribute to the needs of God's people, and welcome strangers into your home. [14]Bless people who harass you—bless and don't curse them. [15]Be happy with those who are happy, and cry with those who are crying. [16]Consider everyone as equal, and don't think that you're better than anyone else. Instead, associate with people who have no status. Don't think that you're so smart. [17]Don't pay back anyone for their evil actions with evil actions, but show respect for what everyone else believes is good. [18]If possible, to the best of your ability, live at peace with all people. (CEB)

1. What are some good skills in getting along with others that you learned from your family? What are some bad habits you learned?

2. What does it mean to love God with our heart? With our soul? With our mind?

3. When Jesus said to love your neighbor, did he mean only the person who has a house next to you? Who else is included in that command?

4. What are some ways you need to live in peace with others? What changes do you need to make for this to happen?

CREATE A NEW STORY

GOD INVITES YOU TO BE PART OF THE KINGDOM—TO WEAVE YOUR STORY INTO GOD'S STORY. THAT WILL MEAN CHANGE. IT WILL REQUIRE YOU TO GO GOD'S WAY RATHER THAN YOUR OWN. THIS WON'T HAPPEN OVERNIGHT, BUT IT SHOULD HAPPEN STEADILY. BY MAKING SMALL, SIMPLE CHOICES, WE CAN BEGIN TO CHANGE OUR DIRECTION. THE HOLY SPIRIT HELPS US ALONG THE WAY—GIVING US GIFTS TO SERVE THE BODY, OFFERING US INSIGHTS INTO SCRIPTURE, AND CHALLENGING US TO LOVE NOT ONLY THOSE AROUND US BUT THOSE FAR FROM GOD.

In this section, talk about how you will apply the wisdom you've learned in this session.

1. In what areas of connecting with others would you get a "smiley face" right now? How about a "frowny face"?

2. How does loving God with our heart, soul, and mind help us love others?

3. How does our treatment of others reflect our relationship with God?

4. What should we do if it's not possible to live in peace with someone because of his or her choices?

> SPEND SOME TIME PRAYING ABOUT THOSE YOU KNOW WHO MIGHT RESPOND TO A SIMPLE INVITATION: TO COME TO A CHURCH SERVICE, TO JOIN YOUR SMALL GROUP, OR EVEN JUST TO HAVE COFFEE AND TALK ABOUT SPIRITUAL MATTERS. ASK THE HOLY SPIRIT TO BRING TO MIND PEOPLE YOU CAN PRAY FOR.

- A strong group is made up of people who are all being filled up by God so that they are empowered to love each other. What specific steps will you take this week to connect with God privately so God can "fill you up?" If you've focused on prayer in past weeks, maybe you'll want to direct your attention to scripture this week. If you've been reading God's word consistently, perhaps you'll want to take it deeper and try memorizing a verse. Tell the group which one you plan to try this week. Then, at your next meeting, talk about your progress and challenges.

- To close your time together, spend some time worshipping God together—praying, singing, and/or reading scripture.

- Have someone use their musical gifts to lead the group in a worship song. Try singing a capella, using a worship CD, or having someone accompany your singing with a musical instrument.

> A strong group is made up of people who are all being filled up by God.

- Choose a psalm or other favorite verse, and read it aloud together. Make it a time of praise and worship as the words remind you of all God has done for you.

- Ask, "How can we pray for you this week?" Invite everyone to share, but don't force the issue. Be sure to write prayer requests on your Prayer Requests and Praise Reports sheet on page 85.

- Close your meeting with prayer.

EXPLORE THE BIBLE PASSAGES
RELATED TO THIS SESSION'S THEME
ON YOUR OWN, JOTTING YOUR
REFLECTIONS IN A JOURNAL
OR IN THIS STUDY GUIDE. YOU
MAY EVEN WANT TO USE A
BIBLE WEBSITE OR APP TO
LOOK UP COMMENTARY ON
THESE PASSAGES.

DIGGING DEEPER

Read Romans 12:10-17

¹⁰*Love each other like the members of your family. Be the best at showing honor to each other.* ¹¹*Don't hesitate to be enthusiastic—be on fire in the Spirit as you serve the Lord!* ¹²*Be happy in your hope, stand your ground when you're in trouble, and devote yourselves to prayer.* ¹³*Contribute to the needs of God's people, and welcome strangers into your home.* ¹⁴*Bless people who harass you—bless and don't curse them.* ¹⁵*Be happy with those who are happy, and cry with those who are crying.* ¹⁶*Consider everyone as equal, and don't think that you're better than anyone else. Instead, associate with people who have no status. Don't think that you're so smart.* ¹⁷*Don't pay back anyone for their evil actions with evil actions, but show respect for what everyone else believes is good. (CEB)*

1. This passage lists a variety of instructions for how Christians should live. Which ones are most difficult for you? Which ones are easiest?

2. How do we bless those who treat us badly or hurt us?

3. Why is it important to rejoice and mourn with those experiencing those emotions?

4. What does it mean to repay evil? Why is it important to avoid this?

Read Psalm 133

¹Look at how good and pleasing it is
when families live together as one!
²It is like expensive oil poured over the head,
running down onto the beard—
Aaron's beard!—
which extended over the collar of his robes.
³It is like the dew on Mount Hermon
streaming down onto the mountains of Zion,
because it is there that the LORD has commanded the blessing:
everlasting life. (CEB)

1. What does it mean for God's people to live in unity?

2. What are we to make of the strange comparison in verse 2? (This might be a great time to check a Bible commentary!)

3. What are some ways God blesses people when they live this way?

DAILY DEVOTIONS

Day 1 • Read Romans 14:19

So let's strive for the things that bring peace and the things that build each other up. (CEB)

Respond:

Does treating other people well mean that you must not treat yourself with care? How can we move toward "build[ing] each other up" in our relationships?

My Action Steps: ....

Day 2 • Read Proverbs 19:11

Insightful people restrain their anger; their glory is to ignore an offense. (CEB)

Respond:

Again, the point here is not that we become doormats but that being a loving, wise person means we also don't make every small problem a major issue. Ask God to help you develop more patience in your relationships and determine what offenses you should overlook.

My Action Steps: ....

Day 3 • Read Philippians 2:14-15

Do everything without grumbling and arguing so that you may be blameless and pure, innocent children of God surrounded by people who are crooked and corrupt. (CEB)

Respond:

How does our willingness to follow God's ways—in this case, watching our tongues—testify to those around us?

My Action Steps: ....

Day 4 • Read Proverbs 17:14

The start of a quarrel is like letting out water, so drop the dispute before it breaks out. (CEB)

Respond:

Wow, is this true or what?! So often a small argument can become a major fight. Are there things you need to "drop" in order to pursue a more peaceful relationship with someone?

My Action Steps: ....

Day 5 • Read Matthew 7:5

You deceive yourself! First take the log out of your eye, and then you'll see clearly to take the splinter out of your brother's or sister's eye. (CEB)

Respond:

We are often quick to find fault with others while excusing our own mistakes. What are the "logs" you need to remove? Ask God to help you identify these issues and work on them.

My Action Steps: ....

Day 6

Use the following space to write any thoughts God has put in your heart and mind about the things we have looked at in this session and during your Daily Devotions time this week.

....

....

....

....

....

DOING GOD'S WILL

But anyone who needs wisdom should ask God, whose very nature is to give to everyone without a second thought, without keeping score. Wisdom will certainly be given to those who ask.

James 1:5 CEB

Have you ever wished you could just e mail God, or send a text, and ask for the answer to a specific question? The Bible gives us many, many insights for living meaningful and joyful lives, but it doesn't give us personal guidance to particular questions: "Who should I marry?" "Should I marry at all?" "What kind of work would use my gifts and talents?" "Where should I live?" "Should I buy this car or that car?" "How many children should I have?" If you ask these questions, you won't find the answer in scripture.

However, God does make a startling promise to us in the book of James—a promise that if we sincerely ask, God will give us God's wisdom. This isn't as easy as getting a text from God telling you what to do, but it is a direct "hotline" to God and a way we can make better choices and live in ways that honor God. This week we'll explore what it means to seek God's will and how we can access the gift of God's wisdom.

SHARE YOUR STORY

Open your group with prayer. This should be a brief, simple prayer in which you invite God to be with you as you meet. You can pray for specific requests at the end of the meeting, or stop momentarily to pray if a particular situation comes up during your discussion.

As we have said in previous lessons, sharing our personal stories builds deeper connections among group members. Your story may be exactly what another person needs to hear to encourage or strengthen them. And your listening to others' stories is an act of love and kindness to them—and could very well help them grow spiritually. Begin your time together by using the following questions and activities to get people talking.

1. What surprised you most about this group? Where did God meet you over the last six weeks?

2. You can have one wish—what would it be? (No wishing for more wishes!)

3. Can you think of a public figure or a celebrity who was blessed with many advantages but destroyed his or her life? What bad choices caused his or her downfall?

WATCH
THE
DVD

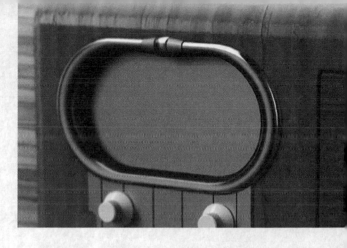

WATCH THE DVD FOR THIS SESSION NOW. USE THIS SPACE TO RECORD KEY THOUGHTS, QUESTIONS, AND THINGS YOU WANT TO REMEMBER OR FOLLOW UP ON. AFTER YOU FINISH WATCHING THE VIDEO, HAVE SOMEONE READ THE DISCUSSION QUESTIONS IN THE HEAR GOD'S STORY SECTION AND DIRECT THE DISCUSSION AMONG THE GROUP. AS YOU GO THROUGH EACH OF THE SUBSEQUENT SECTIONS, ASK SOMEONE ELSE TO READ THE QUESTIONS AND DIRECT THE DISCUSSION.

HEAR GOD'S STORY

After viewing the DVD Session, use the following questions to guide your discussion of the teaching you just experienced in the video, and this Bible passage from James.

READ JAMES 1:2-5

[2]My brothers and sisters, think of the various tests you encounter as occasions for joy. [3]After all, you know that the testing of your faith produces endurance. [4]Let this endurance complete its work so that you may be fully mature, complete, and lacking in nothing. [5]But anyone who needs wisdom should ask God, whose very nature is to give to everyone without a second thought, without keeping score. Wisdom will certainly be given to those who ask. (CEB)

1. We can't ask God for wisdom if we don't think we need it. Take a few minutes to evaluate your life. In what areas do you need God's wisdom and help?

2. Solomon asked God for the ability to tell the difference between right and wrong. What makes that such an important part of wisdom?

3. How can wealth and success make us vulnerable?

4. In the video, Jim said Solomon was "educated beyond his obedience." He knew what to do, but he didn't do it. In what ways does this describe our life? Are there areas in which you are not doing what you know you should do?

5. Solomon's final conclusion in life is to love God and obey the Lord. How would your life change if you made this the goal of your life?

CREATE A NEW STORY

Think about specific steps you want to take to live a new story and to walk more closely with God so you can be part of the story, engaged in God's kingdom.

1. How has God changed your story during this six-week study? What new things is God asking you to do? What truth has transformed your heart?

2. As you walk forward in your relationship with God, what will you do differently as a result of what you've experienced in this group?

3. Jim and Jen shared the story of King Solomon, who followed God for a while and experienced great blessings before he began depending on himself instead. In what areas are you relying on your own wisdom instead of God's?

4. What's the difference between knowing God's commandments and following them? Which is easier? Which pleases God more?

5. In Romans 7 Paul writes that he is exhausted with himself. He says, *"I don't know what I'm doing, because I don't do what I want to do. Instead, I do the thing that I hate. . . . I don't do the good that I want to do, but I do the evil that I don't want to do" (vv. 15, 19).* Do you have an area of your life that continues to trip you up?

6. In what one area of your life do you most want wisdom and guidance?

7. As this is the last meeting in this study, take some time to celebrate the work God has done in the lives of group members. Have each person in the group share some step of growth they have noticed in another member. (In other words, no one will talk about themselves. Instead, affirm others in the group.) Make sure each person gets affirmed and noticed and celebrated—whether the steps they've made are large or small.

8. Review your Community Group Covenant on page 80 and evaluate how well you met your goals. Discuss any changes you want to make as you move forward. If you plan to continue meeting, and your group starts a new study, this is a great time to take on a new role or change roles of service in your group. What new role will you take on? If you are uncertain, perhaps your group members have some ideas for you. Remember, you aren't making a lifetime commitment to the new role; it will only be for a few weeks. Maybe someone would like to share a role with you if you don't feel ready to serve solo.

9. Close by praying about your prayer requests, and take a couple of minutes to review the praises you have recorded over the past five weeks on the Prayer Requests and Praise Reports sheet on page 85.

> If your group still needs to make decisions about continuing to meet after this session, have that discussion now. Talk about what you will study, who will lead, and where and when you will meet.

EXPLORE THE BIBLE PASSAGES RELATED TO THIS SESSION'S THEME ON YOUR OWN, JOTTING YOUR REFLECTIONS IN A JOURNAL OR IN THIS STUDY GUIDE. YOU MAY EVEN WANT TO USE A BIBLE WEBSITE OR APP TO LOOK UP COMMENTARY ON THESE PASSAGES.

Read Psalm 119:97-105

⁹⁷I love your Instruction! I think about it constantly. ⁹⁸Your commandment makes me wiser than my enemies because it is always with me. ⁹⁹I have greater insight than all my teachers because I contemplate your laws. ¹⁰⁰I have more understanding than the elders because I guard your precepts. ¹⁰¹I haven't set my feet on any evil path so I can make sure to keep your word. ¹⁰²I haven't deviated from any of your rules because you are the one who has taught me. ¹⁰³Your word is so pleasing to my taste buds—it's sweeter than honey in my mouth! ¹⁰⁴I'm studying your precepts—that's why I hate every false path.
¹⁰⁵Your word is a lamp before my feet and a light for my journey. (CEB)

1. What is the "law" referred to in this passage? Why is it so important to the psalmist?

2. What action seems necessary to fully understand the wisdom of God's word? (see verses 97 and 99)

3. What is required in addition to knowledge if we are going to gain understanding? (see verses 100 and 101)

4. Why does the author compare God's word to a light or a lamp?

Read James 1:5-8

⁵But anyone who needs wisdom should ask God, whose very nature is to give to everyone without a second thought, without keeping score. Wisdom will certainly be given to those who ask. ⁶Whoever asks shouldn't hesitate. They should ask in faith, without doubting. Whoever doubts is like the surf of the sea, tossed and turned by the wind. ⁷People like that should never imagine that they will receive anything from the Lord. ⁸They are double-minded, unstable in all their ways. (CEB)

1. As you think of the legacy you'd like to pass on, what role does wisdom play in achieving that goal?

2. How can we as individuals, a church, and a country seek wisdom?

3. It's interesting that James, Jesus's brother, writes this. Yet, James did not recognize Jesus as his Lord at first. How have you "missed" Jesus in the past?

DAILY DEVOTIONS

Day 1 • Read 1 Thessalonians 5:16-18

Rejoice always. Pray continually. Give thanks in every situation because this is God's will for you in Christ Jesus. (CEB)

Respond:

Sometimes we ignore the general will of God in our desire for specific insights. Are you rejoicing, praying, and giving thanks?

My Action Steps:

Day 2 • Read James 3:17

What of the wisdom from above? First, it is pure, and then peaceful, gentle, obedient, filled with mercy and good actions, fair, and genuine. (CEB)

Respond:

Do any of these descriptions of wisdom surprise you? Have you seen examples of this from times God has given you wisdom in your own life?

My Action Steps:

Day 3 • Read 1 Peter 2:15-16

It's God's will that by doing good you will silence the ignorant talk of foolish people. Do this as God's slaves, and yet also as free people, not using your freedom as a cover-up for evil. (CEB)

Respond:

How does doing good "silence" those who are opposed to God? Is there a situation in your life that would be improved by following God and submitting to God's will?

My Action Steps: ....

Day 4 • Read Ecclesiastes 2:26

God gives wisdom, knowledge, and joy to those who please God. But to those who are offensive, God gives the task of hoarding and accumulating, but only so as to give it all to those who do please God. (CEB)

Respond:

What a promise! Take some time today to ask for help in pleasing God so that you can experience God's blessings.

My Action Steps: ....

Day 5 • Read Ephesians 5:15-17

So be careful to live your life wisely, not foolishly. Take advantage of every opportunity because these are evil times. Because of this, don't be ignorant, but understand the Lord's will. (CEB)

Respond:

What does it mean to wisely make the most of every opportunity? Why is this so important in our sinful world?

My Action Steps: ....

Day 6

Use the following space to write any thoughts God has put in your heart and mind about the things we have looked at in this session and during your Daily Devotions time this week.

....

....

....

....

....

....

APPENDICES
RESOURCES TO MAKE YOUR SMALL GROUP EXPERIENCE EVEN BETTER!

FREQUENT QUESTIONS

WHAT DO WE DO AT OUR FIRST COMMUNITY GROUP MEETING?

Have a party! Make it fun. A "get to know you" coffee, meal, or dessert is a great way to launch a new study. You may want to review the Community Group Covenant (page 80), and discuss the names of a few friends you can invite to join your group. Don't jump right into study time. Get to know each other first. Even if you are already close, talk about something that happened that week.

WHERE DO WE FIND NEW PARTICIPANTS FOR OUR COMMUNITY GROUP?

Adding people to a group can be troubling. We get comfortable with each other, and then find it awkward to bring in another relationship. Even new groups of four or five people can sense this intimacy. And groups of friends who have been together will lose a few people but not think to recruit new participants. After your group prays about their purpose, create together a list of people to welcome from your neighborhood, your workplaces, your children's school, your families, the gym, and so on. Each participant would then invite the people on his or her list. Church leaders are also willing to announce that your community group is open and welcoming, or put the list of groups in a bulletin insert.

It's very healthy to remain open and welcoming so that new participants can join your group. Attrition happens in groups as people move to new locations, or take on new leadership roles, or hear the calling into other ministry opportunities. So before the group becomes small, making it at risk of stopping, stay open—God will send interesting people your way. You might meet your best friend forever.

HOW LONG WILL COMMUNITY GROUPS MEET?

Most community groups meet weekly for at least their first five weeks. Every other week can work too. In the early months, try to meet weekly as a group. When life happens or when a job requires someone to miss a meeting, they won't miss a month if the group meets occasionally.

At the end of this community group study, each group member may choose whether to stay in the community group or look for another study. Some groups launch relationships that last many years, and others are temporary signposts on the journey into another group experience. The journey is what matters.

CAN WE DO THIS STUDY ON OUR OWN?

One of the best ways to do this study is not with a full house but with a few friends, coworkers, or neighbors. You may prefer to gather with another couple to walk through this study. Then you can be flexible about other ways to grow deeper in friendship by going to see a movie or going out for dinner. God's spirit is present even when two or three are seeking guidance through the scriptures and in prayer (Matt 18:20).

WHAT IF THIS GROUP IS NOT WORKING FOR US?

Sometimes a group encounters a personality conflict, life-stage difference, geographical distance, varied levels of spiritual maturity, or many other differences. Take a breath and pray for God's guidance. When this five-week study is complete, decide whether your group is a good fit for you. It often takes eight to nine weeks for a small group to bond and appreciate each other, so don't bail out before the five weeks of this study are up—God might have something to teach you. Also, don't run from conflict or prejudge a person or group before you have given them a chance. Have you ever noticed that as soon as a difficult person leaves a group, someone else in the group will take their place! God is still working in your life too!

WHO IS THE LEADER?

Healthy community groups rotate hosts/leaders and homes on a regular basis. By sharing the leadership or hosting, participants can learn their unique gifts and feel satisfaction from their contribution. This study guide and the Holy Spirit can keep things on track even when you rotate discussion leaders. Christ promised to be in your midst when you gather. Ultimately, God is your leader each step of the way.

HOW DO WE HANDLE THE CHILD CARE NEEDS IN OUR GROUP?

Handle child care with sensitive thinking. Ask the group to openly suggest solutions. If one approach does not work, adjust to another. Many groups share the cost of a babysitter (or two), who can watch the kids in a different part of the house or yard. Another option is to use one home for the kids and a second home (close by or a phone call away) for the adults. Or if the group has enough adults, the responsibility can be rotated among the adults for the children, either in the same home or in another home nearby. Kids respond well when they see how other parents care for them. Of course, typically each parent can make their own arrangements for their children. Speak openly with each other about the responsibility and the resolution.

COMMUNITY GROUP COVENANT

OUR PURPOSE
To provide a predictable environment where participants experience authentic community and spiritual growth.

OUR GROUP EXPECTATIONS

- **Showing Up**
  We will make an effort through our presence in each group meeting. We will call or e-mail if we cannot attend or will arrive late. (If the Group Calendar is completed, participants will know when to meet.)

- **Comfortable Environment**
  Participants will be heard and feel loved. They will know this because we listen to each other's answers and judgments with respect. Our replies will be gentle and gracious because we are at different stages of spiritual maturity, and our "imperfections" indicate where we are each under construction, moving on toward a complete and whole life together.

- **Keeping Secrets**
  When participants share private and intimate aspects of their personal life, we will not share this outside the group, and we will avoid gossiping about others outside the group.

- **Healthy Growth**
  Participants will serve others with their God-given gifts, and we will help others in the group discover their own strengths and gifts.

- **Everyone in Ministry**
  Every participant will take on a role or responsibility over time in the group.

- **Rotating Hosts and Homes**
  Each participant is encouraged to host the group in his or her home and rotate the responsibility of facilitating a meeting. (See the Group Calendar on page 81.)

COMMUNITY GROUP CALENDAR

Chart out the details together!

Date	Lesson	Host Home	Dessert/Meal	Leader
	1			
	2			
	3			
	4			
	5			
	6			

Group Project:

Group Social:

COMMUNITY GROUP ROSTER

Name	Phone	E-mail

MEMORY VERSE CARDS

CLIP AND REVIEW

SESSION ONE
We won't hide them from their descendants; we'll tell the next generation all about the praise due the LORD *and his strength.* **Psalm 78:4a CEB**

SESSION TWO
Train yourself for a holy life! **1 Timothy 4:7 CEB**

SESSION THREE
We must search and examine our ways; we must return to the LORD. **Lamentations 3:40 CEB**

SESSION FOUR
The righteous live with integrity; happy are their children who come after them. **Proverbs 20:7 CEB**

SESSION FIVE
If possible, to the best of your ability, live at peace with all people. **Romans 12:18 CEB**

SESSION SIX
But anyone who needs wisdom should ask God, whose very nature is to give to everyone without a second thought, without keeping score. Wisdom will certainly be given to those who ask. **James 1:5 CEB**

Clip and review the memory verses
on the other side of this page.

PRAYER REQUESTS AND
PRAISE REPORTS

	Prayer Requests	Praise Reports	
Session 1			Session 1
Session 2			Session 2
Session 3			Session 3
Session 4			Session 4
Session 5			Session 5
Session 6			Session 6

COMMUNITY GROUP LEADERS

KEY RESOURCES TO HELP YOUR
LEADERSHIP EXPERIENCE
BE THE BEST IT CAN BE

STARTING A NEW COMMUNITY GROUP

New community groups can often grow and multiply because the participants gather with more openness than existing small groups. An "open house" is a particularly good way to meet and break the ice with each other before the first session of a group study. The group can also discuss other persons to invite as the study begins. Discuss what each participant can expect from the group, and start off the right way by praying briefly for each other.

In the Gospels, especially in Matthew and Luke, food around a table with teaching is often in the mix when the disciples and seekers are engaged in learning and growing spiritually. So when launching a new community group, tasty desserts or a basic meal will probably stimulate the joy of doing life together.

Ask the participants to introduce themselves and share how or why they are present in this group. If the participants seem shy, you can ask some leading questions:

- What is the most memorable experience from a vacation?
- What is one thing that you appreciate about your community, town, or city?
- Describe a couple things about your childhood that the participants would not know.

Review the Community Group Covenant and talk about each person's expectations and priorities.

Finally, place an empty seat or two in the middle of your group and encourage the group participants to think about a person who could fill that chair or seat over the next few weeks. Provide postcards and have each participant complete one or two invitations. If you get more people than can fit in a room, split into two rooms for discussion. If more than one discussion group is engaged, at the end of a weekly session, gather the whole group for prayer and sharing something they appreciated about the meeting.

While a kick-off meeting might be skipped by an established or experienced small group, any group will experience awakening and renewal by focusing on the purposes of an outwardly focused community group.

LEADING OR HOSTING A DISCUSSION

- If you are nervous about leading a group discussion, you are a healthy and humble person. God usually speaks through reluctant and ordinary persons. God is already present, working ahead in each life through the means of grace (such as personal prayer or searching the scriptures).

- You have gifts that no one else has in the group. So be yourself and listen. Try to limit your talking time to 20 percent of the discussion so that other partic ipants do 80 percent of the talking.

- You are not alone. Other leaders or good friends can pray for you and prepare with you before the discussion.

- Be ready. Go through the session several times. Listen to the teaching segment for the session on the DVD. Write notes in a Bible or in a journal to listen for what God would speak through you. Don't procrastinate. Prepare before the meeting.

- Get evaluation from the participants. Ask them to send an e-mail or write on cards at the meeting about two or three things they liked from the discussion and one thing that could be improved. Be humble and open to growing as a leader or host.

- Tell your group how this study or group relationships are helping you, personally, draw closer to God and friends. Share your struggles and blessings.

Others will see your example and can relate with their own lives.

- Carefully consider another person whom you will ask to lead the group discussion next week. Ask in person, without putting someone on the spot. This is one of the benefits of a community group. The leaders and participants are the same, not experts, because they can't do life alone either.

10 HOST TIPS

1. Relax! Now, breathe! You can do this, and we're here to help if you get stuck. Remember, God is with you. Pray up, prepare, and be friendly. You can do this! Read Hebrews 13:5.

2. Invite. Now invite some more people to join you for this short five-week journey. You are the key to filling your group. #foundpeoplefindpeople

3. Serve a few snacks. Food helps break the ice. Keep it simple and then share this responsibility weekly with your group members.

4. Prepare for your time together. Preview the DVD, write down your thoughts, and select questions that you feel will work best in your group. #growingpeoplechange

5. Pray for your group members. Follow up with them during the week about the concerns in their lives. Make prayer and reaching out to God a regular part of group life. #worshipisalifestyle

6. Maintain a healthy atmosphere. Don't allow anyone, including yourself, to dominate discussion or fall into gossip. Redirect gently when conversation deviates.

7. Be prepared for questions. As questions arise, don't feel like you have to know all the answers. Just say, "I don't know. Let me check that out." Then contact the church office for some help.

8. Allow silence. When you ask questions, if there is silence for a moment, don't jump in too quickly to rescue. This may just be a sign that people are thoughtful about how to respond.

9. Tackle a mission project together! How can you and your group make a difference in the world? Do it! We'd love to hear your stories about it and see pictures! #savedpeopleservepeople

10. Have fun! Plan to do something in this five-week time outside of the group time together just for fun. It helps build friendships and makes the journey more fun together! #youcan'tdolifealone

ABOUT THE
AUTHORS

JIM & JENNIFER
COWART

In June of 2000, Jim and Jennifer Cowart, along with their young children, Alyssa and Josh, were sent by The United Methodist Church to plant a new church in Middle Georgia. With no congregation, building, or land, the Cowarts began Harvest Church as just an idea from God. That idea has now grown into over 3,000 people each weekend.

From small beginnings in a band room, through five years in a movie theater, to a beautiful forty-three-acre campus on the outskirts of Warner Robins, Harvest Church has seen more than 2,800 people accept Jesus as Savior. (In fact, *Outreach Magazine* included Harvest in their "Top 100 Fastest Growing Churches in America" for 2009, 2010, 2014, and 2015.)

Harvest Church has seen more than 2,800 people accept Jesus as Savior.

The Cowarts take the phrase "every member in ministry" seriously, as they encourage every attender to do three things weekly: serve on a ministry team, attend worship, and join a community group.

Jim is a visionary evangelist and serves at Harvest as lead and founding pastor. Jen is the executive pastor and excels in developing systems of ministry and leadership. Their deep commitment to living out the Great Commandment and Great Commission led them to write their first book, *Start This, Stop That*, which was released in 2013. Jim and Jen approach ministry the way they approach life—with a deep commitment to Christ, each other, and joy in the journey.

DON'T STOP NOW!

KEEP DIGGING INTO GOD'S WORD. THESE STUDIES ARE
AVAILABLE FROM JIM AND JEN COWART,
PUBLISHED BY ABINGDON PRESS.

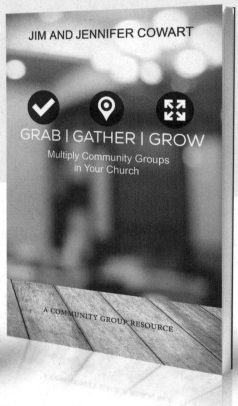